W9-BCO-491

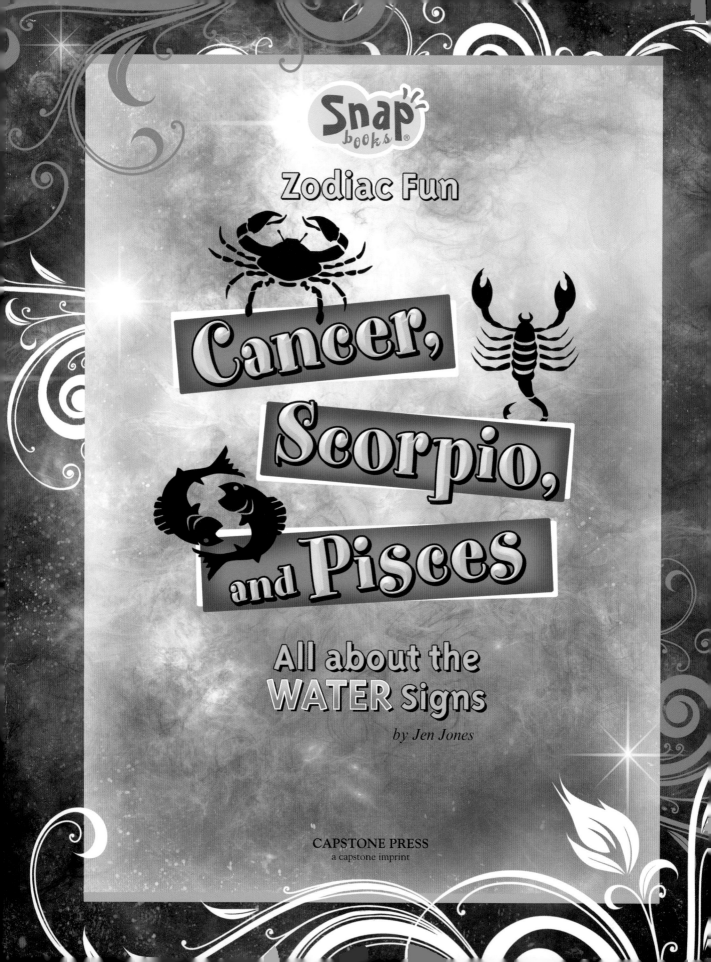

Snap books®

Zodiac Fun

# Cancer, Scorpio, and Pisces

## All about the WATER Signs

by Jen Jones

CAPSTONE PRESS
a capstone imprint

3 1257 01911 6242

Snap Books are published by Capstone Press,
151 Good Counsel Drive, P.O. Box 669, Mankato, Minnesota 56002.
www.capstonepress.com

092009
005618CGS10

Books published by Capstone Press are manufactured with paper
containing at least 10 percent post-consumer waste.

*Library of Congress Cataloging-in-Publication Data*
Jones, Jen.
    Cancer, Scorpio, and Pisces : all about the water signs / by Jen Jones.
    p. cm. — (Snap. Zodiac fun)
    Summary: "Provides information about the water signs of the zodiac" — Provided by publisher.
    Includes bibliographical references and index.
    ISBN 978-1-4296-4015-2 (library binding)
    1. Cancer (Astrology) — Juvenile literature. 2. Scorpio (Astrology) — Juvenile literature. 3. Pisces (Astrology) —
Juvenile literature. 4. Zodiac — Juvenile literature. I. Title. II. Series.
BF1727.3.J66 2010
133.5'2 — dc22                                                                       2009029190

**Editor:** Katy Kudela
**Designer:** Juliette Peters
**Media Researcher:** Jo Miller
**Production Specialist:** Laura Manthe

**Photo Credits:**
Getty Images Inc./Film Magic/Jeff Kravitz, 20; Getty Images Inc./Michael Buckner, 13; Getty Images Inc./WireImage/
Kevin Mazur, 27; iStockphoto/Wilson Valentin, 17 (top left); NASA, 16 (bottom left); NASA/JPL, 23 (bottom left);
NASA/JPL/USGS, 9 (bottom left); Shutterstock/Alex James Bramwell, 10 (top left); Shutterstock/AMP (TW), 22;
Shutterstock/Amy Walters, 17 (bottom); Shutterstock/Ana Vasileva, 26; Shutterstock/Andrejs Pidjass, 18; Shutterstock/
Andrey Chmelyov, 24 (top left); Shutterstock/Baloncici, 4 (top left); Shutterstock/Chris Harvey, 9 (bottom right);
Shutterstock/dhuting, 5; Shutterstock/Dole, 16 (bottom right); Shutterstock/EcoPoint, 9 (top), 19; Shutterstock/fivespots,
16 (top); Shutterstock/James Steidl, 24 (bottom); Shutterstock/Jon Michael Weidman, 12; Shutterstock/Karkas, 10
(top right), 17 (top right), 24 (top right); Shutterstock/Michael Zysman, 11 (both); Shutterstock/openbestdesignstock, 6;
Shutterstock/pdesign, 7 (left), 14 (left), 21 (left); Shutterstock/Pefkos, 8; Shutterstock/Sandra Cunningham, 10 (bottom),
23 (top); Shutterstock/stephan kerkhofs, 25; Shutterstock/Tiplyashin Anatoly, 23 (bottom right); Shutterstock/
Tom Grundy, 15; Shutterstock/ulisse, 7 (right), 14 (right), 21 (right)

**Design Elements:**
Shutterstock/argus; Shutterstock/Epic Stock; Shutterstock/Louisanne; Shutterstock/Mikhail; Shutterstock/pdesign;
Shutterstock/Rashevska Natalila; Shutterstock/sabri deniz kizil; Shutterstock/solos

Essential content terms are bold and are defined at the bottom of the page where they first appear.

# Table of Contents

# Look to the Stars

Fearless or shy. Creative or math-minded. Your personality profile may be written in the stars, sun, moon, and planets. They all play a role in your astrological sign. The day and time you were born also play an important part. In fact, **astrology** says your personality and destiny are formed by the way all these factors line up at birth. Math, astronomy, and mythology are even part of the picture.

How does it all add up? Simply put, astrology is made up of 12 signs. Each sign relates to different months of the year. These signs are grouped into four elements: water, air, earth, and fire. Each element has three signs. Floating under the water element are Cancer, Scorpio, and Pisces.

Doubters don't think astrology has real meaning. After all, how could every Scorpio or every Pisces have the exact same **horoscope**? The truth is that astrology is complicated. Like snowflakes, each person has his or her own unique astrological profile. Though everyone is different, similar qualities are found in people of the same element and sign.

**astrology** — the study of how the positions of stars and planets affect people's lives

**horoscope** — description of personality and future based on an astrological sign

# It's All in the Elements

Take a closer look at the elements. You'll discover just how well each element represents its signs. Water signs are no exception. What makes a Cancer, Scorpio, and Pisces alike? People born under these water signs are deep thinkers. They sometimes get carried away by the waves of their emotions.

## How do water signs mix with other elements?

### Water + Earth

Although this combo makes mud in the great outdoors, it makes a great match for people. The stable earth signs help ground the dreamy water signs. Water signs return the favor by drawing out the emotions of the earth signs.

### Water + Fire

Is water doomed to put out fire's flame? Sure, some water and fire signs don't mesh. But sometimes they are good for each other. Water teaches fire to be more aware of others' needs. Fire asks water to try new ideas and projects.

### Water + Air

Air signs are great at communicating. Water signs often feel deep emotions but keep them private. With an air sign's help, water signs can learn to put their feelings into words.

# Dive In

The three water signs share a lot in common.
But each water sign has its own special traits too.

| **Cancers** are sensitive and caring. | **Scorpios** are fiery and strong. | **Pisces** are thoughtful dreamers. |

Take the plunge to get the inside scoop on each sign.

trait — a characteristic that makes a person stand out from others

*If your birthday falls*
## June 21 through July 22,
*your sign is*

# Cancer

## A Balanced Sign

The Cancer **glyph** looks like two sideways 9s. These symbols are known as "Circle of Spirit" and "Crescent of Soul." The glyph shows the Cancer's need for balance and close friendships.

## Hard to Crack

It's not surprising that Cancer is a water sign. The crab is the sign's aqua-loving animal. Much like a crab, Cancer girls may have a hard outer shell. They choose to keep their emotions inside.

**glyph** — a symbolic character

## Personality Profile:
### The Real Deal on Cancer

● Calm, cool, and collected is the name of the Cancer game.

● Known for their caring nature, Cancers make awesome friends. They are great listeners.

● Cancers are super-sensitive. They feel emotions deeply. Cancers sometimes feel like they are on a rocky roller-coaster ride. Like the twists and turns of a roller coaster, their ever-changing moods can make for lots of ups and downs.

## Personality Pluses

caring
gentle
loyal
smart
trustworthy

## Personality Minuses

easily hurt
guarded
jealous
low confidence
moody

# Just the Facts about Cancer

Lucky day of week: Monday

Part of body ruled: stomach

Flower: larkspur

Ruling planet: Moon

## Style File

Want to be a true Cancer cutie? Dress the part! Cancer's lucky colors are sea green and silver. Be sure to include these soft shades in your wardrobe. If you're feeling dressy, grab a pearl necklace or earrings. After all, pearls are Cancer's lucky stone.

## Cancer Careers

Not sure what to be when you grow up? Let your sign do the talking. Hot careers for a Cancer include social work, human resources, business, and education.

# A Cancer's Social Survival Guide

Did you know that some signs get along better than others? No shocker here, Cancers often click best with other water signs. Find out how the other elements come into play with this quick guide:

## Cancer Friends

Besides Pisces and Scorpio, Cancers have the best chance of being BFF with Taurus, Leo, and Virgo.

## Cancer Foes

Aries is often the worst match for a Cancer. Other possible foes include Capricorn and Libra.

# The Cancer Cast of Characters

## Is Mom or Dad a Cancer?

Lucky you! Cancer is one of the most caring signs in the zodiac. But Cancers also have a hard time with change. Is one of your parents a Cancer? Then try to understand if your mom or dad is bummed that you are growing up. A big event, like getting your driver's license, just might be hard on them.

## Crushin' on a Cancer Cutie?

No need to play hard to get. Cancers like to be told when someone likes them. Don't be afraid to share your crush loud and proud.

**zodiac** — the arrangement of astrological signs that fill a year

# It's All in the Stars:
## Famous Cancers

George W. Bush
Tom Cruise
Princess Diana
Will Ferrell
Selena Gomez

Tom Hanks
Helen Keller
Jessica Simpson
Ashley Tisdale
Prince William

# Selena Gomez

Birthday: July 22, 1992

Selena Gomez starred in the movie *Princess Protection Program*. She's also a star on *Wizards of Waverly Place*. This actress is a true Cancer through and through. Cancers are fiercely loyal to their friends. Selena shows that side with her BFF Demi Lovato. Whether making silly YouTube videos or strutting down the red carpet, this twosome is always attached at the hip.

*If your birthday falls*
## October 23 through November 21,
*your sign is*

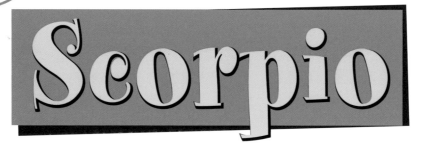
# Scorpio

## A Sassy Sign

The Scorpio glyph looks like a letter "M" with a pointy tail. Scorpio's feisty nature just might mean the "M" stands for "don't mess with me!" Strong and powerful, a Scorpio is almost certain to find success in life.

## Animal Instincts

The name Scorpio comes from the scorpion. It's the sign's ruling animal. Other animals linked with Scorpio are the powerful eagle and the lone wolf.

## Personality Profile:
## The Real Deal on Scorpio

● There's never a dull moment when a Scorpio is around.

● Daring and charming, Scorpios draw others to them like magnets.

● But it's not always fun and games. Sometimes the Scorpio can be a know-it-all.

● No doubt about it, Scorpio is a fierce force. Wherever a Scorpio goes, sizzle follows.

## Personality Pluses

confident
fearless
flirty
full of fire
goal-driven

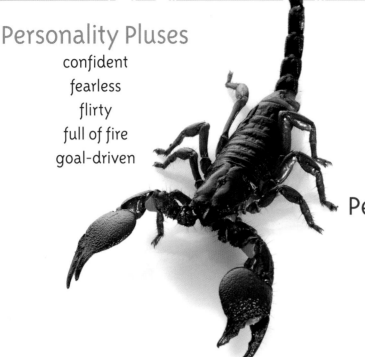

## Personality Minuses

bossy
easily angered
intense
secretive
sometimes selfish

## Just the Facts about Scorpio

Part of body ruled:
reproductive organs

Ruling planet: Pluto

Lucky day of week: Tuesday

Flower: chrysanthemum

# Style File

Scorpios love to wear bold colors. Dark red, maroon, and gold are great picks for the sassy Scorpio gal. For good luck, Scorpios can wear shiny topaz jewelry.

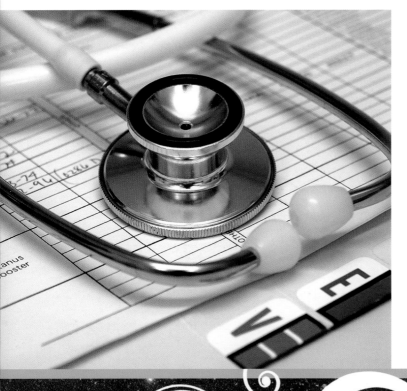

# Scorpio Destiny

High-powered careers are perfect for Scorpios. You'll often see Scorpios taking on jobs like lawyers, police officers, detectives, and doctors. The world of finance is also a great place for Scorpios to use their smarts.

# A Scorpio's Social Survival Guide

Like a magnet, Scorpios pull some signs near and push others away. Most drawn to Scorpio are the other water signs. As for the other signs, find out how Scorpio matches up.

## Scorpio Friends

Scorpios make great leaders. Those who may follow Scorpio's lead include Virgo, Cancer, Pisces, and Capricorn.

## Scorpio Foes

Life can get a bit stormy when a Leo or an Aquarius crosses paths with a Scorpio. Scorpios also don't play well with other Scorpios. These relationships often get too intense.

# The Scorpio Cast of Characters

## Got a Scorpio Sibling?

Beware of the Scorpio sibling. Scorpios are known to hold grudges. You'd better think twice before you borrow your Scorpio sister's iPod without asking. She probably won't forget anytime soon.

## Swooning over a Scorpio?

Dating a Scorpio is always an adventure, but look before you leap. Scorpios can be jealous. They want to know you only have eyes for them. And why wouldn't you? Underneath it all, Scorpios are sweethearts.

# It's All in the Stars:
## Famous Scorpios

| | |
|---|---|
| Prince Charles | Anne Hathaway |
| Hillary Clinton | Kevin Jonas |
| Monique Coleman | Pablo Picasso |
| Leonardo DiCaprio | Julia Roberts |
| Ryan Gosling | Owen Wilson |

## Kevin Jonas

Birthday: November 5, 1987

Scorpios are known for being super-protective. Kevin Jonas is no exception. As the oldest Jonas brother, Kevin looks out for his bandmate bros Nick and Joe on stage and off. Like many Scorpios, he has a playful side and loves to pull pranks.

*If your birthday falls*
# February 19 through March 20,
*your sign is*

# Pisces

## A Sign of Beauty

The Pisces glyph looks like a curly letter "H." Some astrologers think "H" refers to Helen of Troy. A famous character in mythology, Helen was considered one of the world's most beautiful women. If anyone can appreciate beauty, it's a Pisces.

## Fighting the Waves

Two fish swimming in opposite directions is the Pisces' mark. Just like the fish, people born under this sign feel pulled in two directions. Much of the time, they tend to get caught up in a dream world. Yet the demands of the real world often bring them back to reality.

## Personality Profile:
## The Real Deal on Pisces

- If ever there was a daydreamer, it's Pisces.

- Pisces love to get lost in their thoughts.

- Though they enjoy being around people, Pisces crave alone time.

- For a Pisces, inspiration can be found everywhere.

- Pisces are often talented creators of poetry, art, and music.

## Personality Pluses

artistic
creative
full of imagination
kind
spiritual

## Personality Minuses

acts before thinking
a follower
easily discouraged
shy
sometimes spacey

# Just the Facts about Pisces

Part of body ruled: feet

Lucky day of week: Friday

Flower: water lily

Ruling planet: Neptune

# Style File

It's all about bohemian chic for Pisces hippie chicks! Long, flowing fabric is the Pisces' style. They are drawn to water colors like pale green and turquoise. Pisces may top off their look with gold jewelry or aquamarine.

# The Professional Pisces

For this sign of many talents, the sky's the limit. Pisces can explore their creative genius with a career in writing or performing arts. They can also use their generous nature to start a charity or nonprofit organization.

# A Pisces' Social Survival Guide

It's no surprise that Pisces like to swim with other water signs. Of all the fish in the sea, Pisces is happiest with Cancers and Scorpios. Who else floats and rocks Pisces' boat?

## Pisces Friends

Who understands a Pisces' unique outlook on life? An Aries is a good match. A Pisces will also find loyal friends in Taurus and Capricorn.

## Pisces Foes

The Pisces person is often at odds with Gemini. The Gemini's busy pace and high energy can clash with Pisces' "go with the flow" approach. Other caution signs include Virgo and Sagittarius.

# The Pisces Cast of Characters

## Hanging out with a Pisces?

If your pal is a Pisces, you've got a friend for life. Your loyal and loving Pisces friend is happiest with the simple things in life. Heart-to-heart talks will make this friend happy.

## Pining over a Pisces?

Pisces are a mystery. Sometimes it can be a challenge to figure out what they are thinking, so communication is key. If you're a hopeless romantic, the Pisces is right for you.

# It's All in the Stars:
## Famous Pisces

| | |
|---|---|
| Corbin Bleu | Dakota Fanning |
| Cindy Crawford | Shaquille O'Neal |
| Dr. Seuss | Emily Osment |
| Haylie Duff | Queen Latifah |
| Albert Einstein | Carrie Underwood |

# Carrie Underwood

Birthday: March 10, 1983

*American Idol* winner Carrie Underwood has taken the country world by storm. Carrie shows her creative Pisces side by co-writing many of her own songs. When not making top music hits, this southern belle can be found helping others. Carrie shows her compassion through her love for animals. To help out her four-legged friends, she supports charities like People for the Ethical Treatment of Animals (PETA) and the Humane Society.

# Quiz: The Future Looks Bright!

People say your zodiac sign tells a lot about you. But can the stars really guide your career choice? Well, the answers may not be certain, but it sure is fun to think about! No matter the outcome, this quiz will give you plenty of career paths to follow.

**1.** If you could sum yourself up in one word, you'd say you are:

- (A) sensible
- (B) dreamy
- (C) talkative
- (D) energetic

**2.** It's career day. You've arranged to shadow:

- (A) a food critic
- (B) a police officer
- (C) an editor at a local magazine
- (D) a travel agent

**3.** If your friends are looking for you after school, they'll find you:

- (A) setting up for a school dance.
- (B) writing for the school paper.
- (C) practicing with the debate club.
- (D) center stage with the drama club.

**4.** The sky's the limit! Choose the job of your choice:

- (A) party planner
- (B) author
- (C) journalist
- (D) fashion designer

**5.** Assignment alert! Your English teacher dropped a surprise paper. You:

- (A) start researching animal rights topics right after school.
- (B) have the best idea about time travel. It's an A paper for sure... if you ever get around to writing it.
- (C) write a 5-minute protest speech against the food served during school lunches.
- (D) have got a friend who's an excellent writer . . . wink, wink!

**6.** What helps give you your best ideas?

- (A) Time . . . simply time to think is all you need.
- (B) Your ideas are always flowing strongly.
- (C) Talking with your BFFs sparks your brainwaves.
- (D) Biking or running gives you an extra boost of energy to think.

**7.** Your favorite subject in school is:

- (A) social studies
- (B) English
- (C) science
- (D) history

**8.** You're running for student council. You know you could rock the position of:

- (A) treasurer
- (B) secretary
- (C) public relations
- (D) president

**9.** How would your friends best describe you?

- (A) Loyal and honest
- (B) Sweet and caring
- (C) Spontaneous and chatty
- (D) Feisty and charming

**10.** You just landed the best summer job ever! You work:

- (A) at a pet shop.
- (B) at the art gallery.
- (C) as an intern at a local radio station.
- (D) at the laser tag place that just opened.

# Zodiac Chart

| Aries | Leo | Sagittarius |
|---|---|---|
| **March 21–April 19** <br> Fire <br> brave <br> confident <br> energetic | **July 23–August 22** <br> Fire <br> dignified <br> generous <br> playful | **November 22–December 21** <br> Fire <br> adventurous <br> cheerful <br> fun |
| **Taurus** <br> **April 20–May 20** <br> Earth <br> friendly <br> loyal <br> trustworthy | **Virgo** <br> **August 23–September 22** <br> Earth <br> helpful <br> observant <br> practical | **Capricorn** <br> **December 22–January 19** <br> Earth <br> determined <br> hardworking <br> wise |
| **Gemini** <br> **May 21–June 20** <br> Air <br> clever <br> curious <br> lively | **Libra** <br> **September 23–October 22** <br> Air <br> charming <br> fair <br> polite | **Aquarius** <br> **January 20–February 18** <br> Air <br> daring <br> honest <br> independent |
| **Cancer** <br> **June 21–July 22** <br> Water <br> caring <br> gentle <br> sensitive | **Scorpio** <br> **October 23–November 21** <br> Water <br> confident <br> fearless <br> flirty | **Pisces** <br> **February 19–March 20** <br> Water <br> artistic <br> creative <br> kind |

## Quiz Key

When scoring your answers, **A** equals 1 point, **B** equals 2 points, **C** equals 3 points, and **D** equals 4 points. Add them up to discover which element fits you best!

**35–40** = A **fire** signs career might just light up your world! You may enjoy a career in politics, public relations, or even travel.

**26–34** = An **air** signs job might breeze your way! You may enjoy a career as a lawyer, scientist, or even a journalist.

**16–25** = A **water** signs career might wave you down. You may enjoy a career as a teacher, writer, or even a detective.

**10–15** = An **earth** signs job will help you to bloom wherever you are. You may enjoy a career as a real estate agent, a banker, or a chef.

# Glossary

**astrology** (uh-STROL-uh-jee) — the study of how the positions of stars and planets affect people's lives

**astronomy** (uh-STRAH-nuh-mee) — the study of stars, planets, and other objects in space

**destiny** (DESS-tuh-nee) — your fate or future events in your life

**element** (EL-uh-muhnt) — one of the four categories of signs found in the zodiac; the elements are air, earth, fire, and water.

**glyph** (GLIF) — a symbolic character; each of the 12 astrology signs has individual glyphs.

**horoscope** (HOR-uh-skope) — a reading of the position of the stars and planets and how they might affect a person's life

**mythology** (mi-THOL-uh-jee) — a collection of myths

**trait** (TRATE) — a quality or characteristic that makes one person different from another

**unique** (yoo-NEEK) — one of a kind

**zodiac** (ZOH-dee-ak) — the arrangement of astrological signs that fill a year, beginning and ending in March

# Read More

**Aslan, Madalyn.** *What's Your Sign? A Cosmic Guide for Young Astrologers.* New York: Grosset & Dunlap, 2002.

**Jones, Jen.** *Fashion Careers: Finding the Right Fit.* The World of Fashion. Mankato, Minn.: Capstone Press, 2007.

**Marks, Jennifer.** *Aries, Leo, and Sagittarius: All About the Fire Signs.* Zodiac Fun. Mankato, Minn.: Capstone Press, 2010.

# Internet Sites

FactHound offers a safe, fun way to find Internet sites related to this book. All of the sites on FactHound have been researched by our staff.

Here's all you do:

Visit *www.facthound.com*

FactHound will fetch the best sites for you!

# Index

# About the Author

A Los Angeles-based author, **Jen Jones** has written more than 35 books for Capstone Press. (Born on August 3rd, she's a proud Leo lioness!) Along with writing books, Jen has published stories in magazines such as *American Cheerleader, Dance Spirit, Ohio Today,* and *Pilates Style.* In the past, she was a staff writer for *E! Online* and *PBS Kids,* as well as a Web site producer for major talk shows such as *The Jenny Jones Show, The Sharon Osbourne Show,* and *The Larry Elder Show.* Jen is also a member of the Society of Children's Book Writers and Illustrators.